Birds of Evergrene

Third Edition*

Alan Rubin and Greg Braun

*The 3rd Edition of this book includes 28 new bird species and 102 new photos that were not included in the 1st Edition that was published in 2021.

Photo Acknowledgements

All 170 photos in this book were taken in Evergene (over 85% of which were taken by Alan Rubin).

The following photos were taken by Greg Braun: Eastern Phoebe, Eastern Towhee, Red-eyed Vireo, Black-and-white Warbler, Palm Warbler, adult Bald Eagle, Broad-winged Hawk, Red-shouldered Hawk, Eastern Screech Owl, Swallow-tailed Kite, and Southern Flying Squirrel.

The following photos were taken by LeRoy Tabb, seasonal Evergrene resident and bird enthusiast: Gray-headed Swamphen, Magnificent Frigatebird, Least Sandpiper, Wilson's Snipe, Cedar Waxwing, Northern Parula, Yellow-bellied Sapsucker, and immature Bald Eagle.

Table of Contents

Introduction

Evergrene is a residential community located in Palm Beach Gardens in southeastern Florida (see map in Appendix 1). It was the first residential development in the state of Florida to be designated an Audubon Signature Sanctuary (gold level) by Audubon International. Evergrene received its first certification in 2003 when the community was first established. This certification has been recertified annually ever since. This rare honor recognizes the extent to which sustainable designs and construction methods were used in the development of the community. It also recognizes Evergrene as a leader in management practices that maintain a clean and safe environment for people, pets, and wildlife.

Evergrene encompasses approximately 360 acres that include over 50 acres of permanently protected preserves, wetlands, lakes, ponds, and canals. At the heart of Evergrene is Lake Dorothy (see map in Appendix 2), a 37-acre lake that is surrounded by wide sidewalks where residents enjoy biking, jogging, or walking. Evergrene's wooded preserves and quiet waterways offer a perfect environment for the diverse species of birds and other wildlife that live or migrate to our community. More than 115 species of birds have been documented in Evergrene, and 87 are included in this book (see Appendix 3, Evergrene Bird List.)

As part of its involvement in Audubon International's Cooperative Sanctuary Program, Evergrene installed and maintains nest boxes to enhance the nesting habitat for native species. Ten nest boxes were initially installed in 2003. This number grew to 36 in 2024. (Appendix 2 shows the locations of the boxes.) The nest boxes are built in a variety of shapes and sizes to accommodate the nesting of various bird species in the community. These boxes help to maintain nesting populations of screech owls, wood ducks, woodpeckers, and a variety of other wildlife, including flying squirrels.

The birds of Evergrene live the good life – swimming, catching fish, building homes, and raising youngsters. This book is intended to help residents become familiar with the birds that share our neighborhood. Most of the species featured in this book can also be found in other areas of southeastern Florida, so this book would be useful for other residents and visitors to the area. Bird species are separated into the general categories of Water and Wetland Birds, Land Birds, and Raptors. Within these categories, species are arranged in alphabetical order.

Water and Wetland Birds

Anhinga

Anhingas often perch near the water's edge where they spread out their striking black-and-white wings to dry. They swim with their bodies under water. Their long necks extend out of the water, giving them a snake-like appearance (see bottom photo).   Anhingas find food in the water by stalking fish and spearing them with their long, sharp bills. Male Anhingas have black heads and necks. Female Anhingas appear similar to the males but have brown feathers on their heads and necks.

Anhinga, Male

Anhinga, Female

Black-necked Stilt
The Black-necked Stilt's long thin bill, extremely long legs, and black-and-white plumage make this graceful wetland bird easily recognizable. Stilts are present in south Florida throughout the year but are infrequently seen in Evergrene. They may be spotted during the springtime dry season near low water levels and in shallow mud flats along the edges of wetlands.

Brown Pelican
Brown Pelicans are large, stocky seabirds with thin necks and very long bills. They soar above the water looking for prey. When they spot a fish, they dive down. As they hit the water surface, the impact of their large bodies stuns the fish, which they scoop up in their expandable throat pouches. When not foraging for food, pelicans stand near the water, such as on the pier at Lake Dorothy. Brown Pelicans are more often seen in coastal saltwater areas than in freshwater habitats. They are year-round residents in Florida.

Coots and Gallinules

American Coot

American Coots are medium-sized duck-like birds that are easy to identify by their dark bodies and white bills. They are good swimmers and excellent divers, but awkward fliers. These omnivores sometimes steal food from other birds. They are mostly seen on the lake in Evergrene, but they may be found in other open waters where they forage on aquatic plants. They live in small flocks and are migratory, arriving annually in the fall and staying through the spring.

Common Gallinule

Closely related to Coots, Common Gallinules are medium-sized water birds that have red foreheads, yellow-tipped bills, and white patches on both sides of their tail. Common Gallinules are sometimes called Moorhens. They can swim better than they can fly. Year-round residents in Evergrene, Gallinules nest in the late spring and early summer in the dense vegetation along wetland and

Gray-headed Swamphen

Related to Florida's native Common Gallinules, Purple Gallinules, and American Coots, Gray-headed Swamphens are relatively recent additions to Florida's wetland birds. Their larger size, bright red bill and frontal red shield make this species readily identifiable. They are only occasionally seen in Evergrene where they may be hidden amid dense vegetation along the edges of wetlands and lakes.

Purple Gallinule

Purple Gallinules have purple, green, and blue bodies with a pale blue shield on their forehead and a bright red and yellow bill. Their vivid colors make them easy to identify. These year-round residents of Florida are infrequently seen in Evergrene. They may be found in dense vegetation along the shore of wetlands and lakes.

Double-crested Cormorant

With their dark plumage, Cormorants are somewhat similar in appearance to male Anhingas. However, a close look will differentiate the two. Anhinga's wings are black and white, while Cormorants are all black. In addition, Cormorants have down-turned hooks at the end of their beaks. Anhingas' beaks are straight. Cormorants are year-round residents in Evergrene.

Ducks

Black-bellied Whistling Duck

Relatively uncommon newcomers to Evergrene, whistling ducks get their name from their characteristic call, most often heard in the evenings as they fly to overnight roosts. They are relatively large ducks with bright red-orange bills. Sometimes 40 to 50 ducks have been seen at one time in Evergrene.

Blue-winged Teal

Blue-winged Teals are somewhat smaller than other ducks in Florida. The male's white crescent between its bill and eyes and the blue wing patch are features that distinguish this species from other ducks. They are primarily plant eaters and are typically found in small flocks on shallow, open water areas where there is access to aquatic plants. Blue-winged Teals migrate long distances, leaving their northern breeding grounds in the fall and remaining in southern Florida through the spring.

Blue-winged Teal, Male

Blue-winged Teal, Female

Lesser Scaup

The striking black, gray, and white plumage of adult male Lesser Scaup differ from the brown plumage of most other ducks in Evergrene. These ducks prefer large bodies of open water. Flocks of up to 70 Lesser Scaup have been seen on Lake Dorothy in the winter. They migrate in the spring to nesting sites as far away as Canada and Alaska.

Mottled Duck

Sometimes called the Florida duck, Mottled Ducks are the most common duck in Evergrene. These non-migratory ducks are typically seen throughout the year in groups of two to ten. They nest annually in Evergrene during the late spring and early summer. Urbanization and drainage of wetlands have reduced their available habitat in many areas. They are threatened by crossbreeding with Mallards who are close relatives.

8

Northern Shoveler

Northern Shovelers are large ducks with a significantly oversized bill in proportion to the rest of its body. The males have rich chestnut plumage on both sides. Females are more drab brown. Northern Shovelers nest across the northern U.S. to Alaska. They are occasionally seen in Evergrene, but only during the winter months.

Ring-necked Duck

Ring-necked Ducks seem as though they should be named ring-billed ducks, because the white ring around their dark bills is far more noticeable than the cinnamon ring at the base of their necks. Males are black and white, and females are varying shades of brown. The distinctive white rings on their bills and uniformly dark upper wings distinguish male Ring-necked Ducks from Lesser Scaup. A migratory species that nests across northern North America, flocks of Ring-necked Ducks are occasionally seen on Lake Dorothy in the winter.

Ruddy Duck

Ruddy Ducks are small, compact ducks with stout, scoop-shaped bills and long stiff tails that are often pointed upward. They dive to feed on aquatic invertebrates, mostly at night. Ruddy Ducks are occasionally seen in Evergrene during the winter. You might see them sleeping during the daytime on Lake Dorothy as they float with their heads tucked backward under a wing. They are a migratory species that nests across the northern U.S.

Wood Duck - Male

Male Wood Ducks are very colorful with multi-colored bodies; green, black, purple, and white heads; red eye rings; and red, yellow, and black bills. They are year-round residents in Evergrene and frequently occupy nest boxes during the springtime nesting season.

Wood Duck - Female

Female Wood Ducks are less flamboyant than their male counterparts. They are primarily gray, with blue on the back of their wings and white around their eyes. They nest in tree cavities and nest boxes where they lay up to a dozen golf-ball-size eggs during the spring nesting season. They occasionally lay eggs in the nests of other birds.

Egrets

Three species of Egrets are found in Evergrene – Cattle Egrets, Great Egrets, and Snowy Egrets. Great Egrets and Snowy Egrets are similar in appearance, but there are several distinguishing features that help tell them apart. Great Egrets are larger with yellow bills and black legs and feet. Snowy Egrets are smaller with black bills, black legs, and yellow feet. Cattle Egrets are even smaller and have short yellow bills. All three species have lacy plumes during the breeding season.

Cattle Egret

Unlike other Egrets that are wading birds, the all-white Cattle Egret forages for lizards, grasshoppers, and other prey in open grassy areas. Cattle Egrets get their name from their habit of following cattle to catch their prey. In urbanized Florida, they are more well-known for following behind lawn mowers.

Great Egret

Great Egrets are one of several species of white wading birds that are often seen searching for aquatic prey along the shorelines of Evergrene's lakes, ponds, and canals. They are about 3 feet tall with a yellow bill and black stick-like legs. Their dazzling snow-white plumage is the same in both males and females. These birds were nearly hunted to extinction in the late 1800's to provide decorative feathers for women's hats. They are seen in Evergrene throughout the year.

Evergrene's logo is an artist's rendering of a Great Egret. There are many plaques around the community with this logo.

Snowy Egret

Snowy Egrets are smaller (approximately 2 feet tall) than Great Egrets. Snowy Egrets' yellow feet and long thin black bills also differentiate them from Great Egrets which have yellow bills. They are thought by some to be the most beautiful of North American Egrets and Herons. Snowy Egrets are year-round residents in Evergrene and are typically seen along the water's edge.

Egyptian Goose

Egyptian Geese are not native to Florida, but they have become established as year-round residents. Their plumage is unmistakable – mostly shades of tan and brown with dark eye patches and a dark ring around their necks. They occasionally may be spotted in Evergrene on open water lakes and ponds or adjacent areas. (For more information about Egyptian Geese, see reference 5 on page 70.)

Greater Yellowlegs

Greater Yellowlegs are approximately 14 inches in height with long bright yellow legs. Their cousins, Lesser Yellowlegs, are very similar in appearance but are somewhat smaller (about 10 inches in height). Both species are occasionally seen along shallow mud flats in coastal and inland areas throughout Florida in the fall, winter, and spring before migrating north for nesting. Yellowlegs are only occasionally observed in Evergrene during the springtime where they forage in shallow pools.

Gulls

Bonaparte's Gull

Bonaparte's Gulls' winter plumage is mostly white with gray upper parts. Their heads are white with a characteristic dark spot behind their eyes and a black bill. Bonaparte's Gulls are smaller than other Gulls. They migrate in the fall from Canada and Alaska to the east and west coasts of the U.S. They are often seen in large flocks at the beach which is where they find their preferred prey such as marine fish and other organisms. When the seas are too rough for them to find prey, they fly inland to bodies of fresh water.

Ring-billed Gull

Various Gulls and Terns often congregate in large numbers on the dock near the clubhouse in Evergrene. This species gets its name from the dark ring around its otherwise yellow-colored bill. Ring-billed Gulls are the most common Gulls in Evergrene. They return from nesting areas in the north during the fall and stay through the spring.

Herons

Great Blue Heron

The Great Blue Heron is the largest Heron native to North America. These stately birds can be up to 4 feet tall with 6-foot wingspans and an S-shaped neck. They have grayish-blue feathers and long dark plumes that extend from just above their eyes to the back of their head. They are experts at fishing, but they can also strike like lightning to grab a mouse, frog, or other prey. Great Blue Herons are year-round residents in Evergrene, but no evidence of nesting has been found. They are frequently observed along the shorelines of Evergrene's wetlands. Their low guttural squawks can occasionally be heard during the night when they have been disturbed.

Green Heron

Green Herons, formerly known as Green-backed Herons, are smaller than most other Herons and Egrets. They have relatively short necks and are approximately 20 inches tall. Due to their camouflage coloring and more secretive ways, they are not seen as often as other wading birds. They are year-round residents in Evergrene and may be observed hunting for aquatic prey in the vegetation along wetland shorelines.

Little Blue Heron

As implied by their name, Little Blue Herons are smaller than most other Herons. Adults have dagger-like two-toned bills, purple and maroon heads and necks, and dark slate-blue bodies. During their first year, juvenile Little Blue Herons are entirely white. When immature Blue Herons molt into adults, their plumage turns to a patchwork of white and blue. By the time they are two years old, they have most of their dark blue adult plumage. Little Blue Herons are year-round residents in Evergrene and are typically seen foraging along the water's edge.

Adult

Juvenile

Immature

Tricolored Heron

Tricolored Herons are intermediate in size (e.g., larger than Little Blue Herons but smaller than Great Blue Herons). Their gray, purple, and white feathers give this species its common name. Like other Herons and Egrets, Tricolored Herons have long toes which give them the ability to walk on waterlily pads. They are year-round residents in Evergrene and are often seen walking along the perimeter of Evergrene's marshes.

Ibis

Glossy Ibis
The stunning colors of the Glossy Ibis – deep maroon, emerald bronze, and violet – make them very easy to distinguish from the White Ibis. The long, sturdy, down-curved bill of the Glossy Ibis is a perfect tool for probing into wetland soils for crabs, crayfish, and other aquatic organisms. They can occasionally be seen near shallow wetlands in Evergrene.

White Ibis
Flocks of White Ibis are commonly seen along the perimeter of Evergrene's wetlands and on neighborhood lawns. White Ibis frequently coo softly while foraging and use their long, bills to poke into the ground as they search for insects. They are one of Evergrene's most common wading birds and are seen throughout the year, sometimes in flocks of more than 100 birds. Juveniles have brown feathers on top with lighter brown streaky necks. They are white below with orange pink bills.

Juvenile White Ibis

Least Bittern
One of Evergrene's smallest and most secretive wading birds, Least Bitterns are mostly tawny brown. Their habitat is emergent shoreline vegetation where they search for aquatic prey among plant stalks.

Least Tern
Similar to Gulls, Terns are highly adapted for catching live prey – mostly fish. The Least Tern is the smallest of about a dozen species of Terns found in Florida. A migratory species that winters in South and Central America, Least Terns typically arrive in south Florida in March. They are most often seen in small groups in Evergrene over Lake Dorothy or perched on the pier near the clubhouse.

Limpkin

Limpkins are mid-sized wading birds that have dark brown feathers with white flecks. Their name is derived from an apparent limp when they walk. Limpkins have piercing cries that are primarily heard at dawn and dusk but can also be heard in the middle of the night during the springtime courtship and nesting season. They were once abundant in Florida but were almost eradicated by hunters because they are so easy to catch or shoot. Now they are protected by state and Federal laws, and their population in Florida has increased in recent years. Limpkins are year-round residents and are most often observed foraging for apple snails along Evergrene's wetland shorelines.

Magnificent Frigatebird
Magnificent Frigatebirds are large, highly aerodynamic birds that are found mostly over tropical oceans and coastlines. They are rarely seen inland except during periods of strong onshore winds. Their long pointed black wings and forked tails enhance their capability for soaring. Males are all black with a scarlet throat pouch that can be inflated like a balloon during the breeding season.

Pied-billed Grebe
Pied-billed Grebes are small brown, white, and gray duck-like birds that appear to have no tail. They often dive underwater to search for prey, such as crustaceans, small fish, and aquatic plants.

Red-winged Blackbird

The bright red shoulder patches of adult male Red-winged Blackbirds distinguish them from all other black-plumaged birds. The male's plumage differs markedly from the female's, which is streaky dark brown and which lacks the male's bright red shoulder patches. These birds are found across much of North America, from Florida to southern Alaska. They are year-round residents in Evergrene and are most often found near wetlands and along the shore of Lake Dorothy.

Red-winged Blackbird, Female

Red-winged Blackbird, Male

Roseate Spoonbill

The most colorful of the wading birds, Roseate Spoonbills have been seen with increasing regularity in Evergrene in recent years. They use their spoon-shaped bills to sift through the water along Evergrene's waterways as they forage for food. Immature Spoonbills (lower photo) don't get the full color of the adults until they are 2 to 3 years old. Because of their splashy pink color, they are one of the most popular birds that Evergrene residents enjoy seeing.

Sandhill Crane

Sandhill Cranes are large gray birds that stand almost 4 feet tall. Their height and red-crowned heads make them easy to recognize. Sandhill Cranes often dance during both play and courtship, and they mate for life. The males and females have loud trumpeting calls that are hard to miss. They are among the oldest living species of birds. This Florida sub-species has been designated by the State of Florida as a "threatened" species. They are typically seen in or near shallow wetlands, often in pairs or small family groups of three or four. Be careful while driving because they sometimes walk slowly across the road.

Young Sandhill Cranes, called colts, may climb on their mother's back where they have a comfortable spot to sleep while their mother watches over and protects them. At least two families of sandhill cranes reside in Evergrene.

Sandpipers

Least Sandpiper

One group of small Sandpipers is called "peeps" because of the sound they make. Least Sandpipers have yellow legs, a short downward curved bill, and light lines on their head behind their eyes which help distinguish them from other peeps. These migratory shorebirds can be found in Florida from the fall through the spring. Although rarely seen in Evergrene, they may be spotted along shorelines and shallow mud flats during the spring dry season.

Solitary Sandpiper

Solitary Sandpipers have brown plumage with white spots and an obvious white eye-ring. Although many Sandpipers can be found near the ocean, Solitary Sandpipers prefer habitats in interior, freshwater wetlands. These migratory birds nest in the summertime from Canada to Alaska, and they spend winters in Central and South America. They occasionally stop in Evergrene to refuel during their several thousand-mile fall and spring migrations.

Wilson's Snipe

With their brown and white stripes and bars, Wilson Snipes are well camouflaged. It takes a good eye to spot this bird as it sits motionless on the edges of muddy wetlands. Its bill is very long in proportion to the rest of its body which is about 10 inches in total length. Snipes are rarely seen in Evergrene. They reside in the southern U.S. from the fall through the spring before migrating north to nest in the summer.

Wood Stork

Wood Storks are large, mostly white birds, with dark heads and necks, and long bills. When foraging for food along the water's edge, they hold their bills open underwater. When they feel a fish, they slam their beaks shut like a mousetrap. Wood Storks are seen frequently throughout the year in Evergrene. Colonies of Wood Storks nest in the springtime in treetops at Wakodahatchee Wetlands, which is about 30 miles south of Evergrene.

Land Birds

Blue-gray Gnatcatcher
At approximately 4" in length from the tip of its bill to the end of its tail, Blue-gray Gnatcatchers are one of South Florida's smallest birds. These birds are nearly always on the move searching for caterpillars and other small insects, often in the canopy of oak and pine trees. In spite of their name, gnats are not a significant part of their diet. They can be observed regularly in Evergrene from the fall through springtime. Even when they cannot be seen, their low-pitched trill often gives away their presence.

Blue Jay
Blue Jays are one of the first birds that many people learn to identify, so their 11-inch size is a useful benchmark to compare to other birds. They have blue, white, and black plumage with a pronounced crest on their head. Male Blue Jays are indistinguishable from females. Blue Jays are most often detected by their noisy calls. They are common year-round residents in Evergrene.

Brown Thrasher
The Brown Thrasher is one of only eight species of Thrasher that is found in Florida. Although they are year-round residents in Evergrene, Brown Thrashers are not often seen here. Their overall brown appearance, long tails, and white undersides with brown streaks help to identify this medium-sized species. They may be seen on or near the ground along preserve edges as they search for food, which includes insects, small amphibians, fruit, and some seeds.

Cedar Waxwing
These showy birds are unlikely to be confused with any other species. The distinct combination of the Cedar Waxwing's colors, including dark faces, brown crests on the back of their heads, red wing tips, and yellow tips on their tails, make this species easy to identify. A migratory species that nests across the northern U.S. and Canada, these insect and fruit-eaters fly south during the fall, stay throughout the winter, and return north in the spring. They don't maintain territories while they are here, so finding them at Evergrene is mostly a matter of luck and being in the right place at the right time.

Doves

Eurasian Collared-Dove

The Collared-Dove gets its name from the black half-collar at the nape of its neck. Collared-Doves are larger than the more common Mourning Doves, with broad wings and squared-off tails. Not originally found in Florida, this Eurasian species is expanding in numbers and can now be seen throughout most of the U.S. They are year-round residents in Evergrene.

Mourning Dove

Mourning Doves have plump bodies with short legs, small bills, and heads that look small in comparison to their bodies. Mourning Doves get their name from their plaintive, sad songs. They are year-round residents in Evergrene and nest here in late spring and summer.

White-winged Dove

White-winged Doves get their name from the long white stripes along the edges of their wings. The rest of their body is mostly gray. These doves do well in urban settings and are found in the southern U.S. from Florida to California. Although they are year-round residents in Evergrene, they are not commonly seen here. When they are seen, it is most likely around Lake Dorothy.

Eastern Phoebe

Eastern Phoebes are smaller than Cardinals with gray heads, olive-green backs, white undersides, and faint yellow streaks on their bellies that are sometimes difficult to see. They are insect-eating birds that migrate south when cold and snowy weather arrives in their nesting habitats across the northern U.S. and Canada. They return to Florida in the fall and can be found near Evergrene's wetlands through the springtime.

Eastern Towhee

At about 7 inches in length, Eastern Towhees are smaller than Cardinals. They have jet-black backs, warm reddish-brown sides, and white undersides. They are year-round residents in Evergrene. However, they are not commonly seen here because they spend most of their time either concealed in bushes or on the ground in thick underbrush. A small number of Towhees inhabit the pine flatwoods in the vicinity of the pond southwest of the Donald Ross Road entrance to Evergrene.

European Starling

At about 8 inches in length, European Starlings are about the same size as Cardinals. These dark-plumaged, iridescent birds have a bright yellow bill. They have a tenacious disposition and will often take over nests that other species have made. Reportedly introduced to North America in 1890 in New York City, Starlings can now be found in all of the lower 48 states and across most of Canada. They are mostly seen around the Evergrene clubhouse and often nest in holes created by woodpeckers.

Fish Crow

Fish Crows are fairly common in Evergrene. Their guttural "ugh-ugh" call differs from the stereotypical "caw-caw" sound that common Crows make. Fish Crows are smaller than common Crows but have the same dark plumage. They tend to gather in large flocks during the non-nesting months and in smaller family groups during the spring and summer nesting season. Fish Crows are year-round residents at Evergrene.

38

Grackles

Boat-tailed Grackle

Adult male Boat-tailed Grackles have iridescent black plumage and dark bills. The common name of this bird stems from its long, keel-shaped tail. Female Boat-tailed Grackles have shorter tails than males. They have tawny brown coloration over most of their body with darker wings and tails. Boat-tailed Grackles are year-round residents in Evergrene and are frequently seen around the clubhouse snack bar looking for food.

Boat-tailed Grackle, Male

Boat-tailed Grackle, Female

Common Grackle

Common Grackles are smaller and have shorter tails than Boat-tailed Grackles. Another distinguishing feature of Common Grackles is that they have yellow eyes. Common and Boat-tailed Grackles do well in urban areas. They are commonly found in Evergrene, particularly near the clubhouse where they often pilfer scraps of food.

Gray Catbird

Catbirds, which are approximately the size of Cardinals, are mostly gray and black. Named for their cat-like calls, they are migratory birds that nest in northern latitudes. They return to Florida in the fall and stay through the springtime. Catbirds are heard more often than they are seen. They are usually found in dense bushes, but they occasionally venture out into the open to search for berries, including berries from the native dahoon holly and gallberry. Many hollies have been planted in Evergrene to provide food for birds and other native wildlife.

Great Crested Flycatcher

Similar in size to Cardinals, Great Crested Flycatchers have olive-green backs and yellow undersides. They can also be identified by the crest on top of their heads, which may be raised or lowered, depending on the bird's mood. They have a loud clear song and have been observed during the spring and summer in Evergrene's pine flatwood preserves. Although they are year-round residents in South Florida, they are infrequently seen in Evergrene.

House Sparrow

House Sparrows were initially introduced in the 1850's in New York City from Europe but have expanded their range across the entire U.S. and Canada. They are year-round residents in Florida. These omnivores are common in urban areas where they forage for seed grains, caterpillars, and even insects from the grills of vehicles.

Killdeer

Killdeer, which are members of the Plover family, get their name from the shrill "kill-deer" call they make as they fly overhead. Although many Plovers are typically seen on sandy beaches, Killdeer mostly inhabit short grassy inland areas. Killdeer have two black "necklaces" which distinguish them from other Plovers. They run along the ground trying to scare up insect prey. These year-round residents nest on the ground making them fairly uncommon in areas where ground predators (bobcats, foxes, raccoons. dogs. etc.) are found.

Loggerhead Shrike

Approximately 9 inches in length, Loggerhead Shrikes are about the same size as Mockingbirds. They are year-round residents in Evergrene, but they are elusive and not commonly seen. Individuals from a few families that reside in Evergrene may be observed perched in trees around the perimeter of the lake. This masked black, white, and gray predator hunts from high perches, and preys on insects, smaller birds, lizards, and small mammals.

Northern Cardinal

Male Northern Cardinals have brilliant crimson red bodies with black surrounding their bills. They sing in loud clear whistles, most often in the springtime, as they establish and defend nesting territories. Their strong beaks are perfectly adapted for their diet of seeds and berries. Female Northern Cardinals have the same distinctive crests on their heads and reddish-orange beaks as males, but their plumage is mostly pale brown with warm reddish tinges on their wings. This makes them less noticeable while sitting on eggs and raising young. Northern Cardinals reside in Evergrene throughout the year.

Northern Cardinal, Male

Northern Cardinal, Female

Northern Mockingbird

At about 10 inches in length, Northern Mockingbirds are commonly seen in Evergrene throughout the year. They are mostly gray with long dark tails and white stripes on the edges of their wings. They get their name from their unusual ability to mimic songs of other birds and have even been known to imitate the ring of cell phones. The Mockingbird is the state bird of Florida.

Painted Bunting

Painted Buntings are winter-time visitors to South Florida. Males are one of the showiest birds in Evergrene. With their brightly colored red, blue, green, and yellow feathers, male Painted Buntings are a treat to see. Females are less colorful than the males and have yellowish-green plumage. They are attracted to millet seeds in feeders.

Painted Bunting, Male

Painted Bunting, Female

Purple Martin

About 8 inches in length, Purple Martins are the largest species of the Swallow family in Florida. Males are dark iridescent blue, and females are mostly gray with lighter undersides. Purple Martins' favorite prey are insects, including mosquitos. They spend most of the year in Central or South America before they migrate to the U.S. in late winter. They nest in miniature "condominiums" such as the one pictured here that is on the east side of Lake Dorothy.

Ruby-throated Hummingbird

Male ruby-throated Hummingbirds have shimmering ruby throats that flash red if seen from just the right angle. Females (pictured below) are less flashy than males and have white undersides. They feed on nectar and are attracted to native plants with tubular flowers, although they will occasionally come to hummingbird feeders. Hummingbirds are winter-time residents in South Florida and migrate to cooler climates during the summer.

Vireos

Approximately 6 inches in length, Vireos are larger than Warblers and smaller than Blue Jays. About a half-dozen species of Vireos are found in Florida. They feed on insects, worms, and other invertebrates and are most often seen in woodlands and thick forests. They are uncommon winter residents in Evergrene.

Red-eyed Vireo
Red-eyed Vireos have gray crowns, black lines across their eyes, and white stripes above and below the black lines.

White-eyed Vireo
Although several species of Vireo spend the fall and winter in southeast Florida before returning to breeding grounds in northern latitudes, White-eyed Vireos are year-round residents in Evergrene. They usually are found around dense vegetation near wetlands.

Vultures

Black Vulture

Black Vultures and Turkey Vultures are scavengers that feed on carrion. Black Vultures are bare headed with black plumage on the rest of their bodies. They have hooked bills, broad wings, and short tails. Black Vultures make up for their poor sense of smell by following Turkey Vultures to carcasses.

Turkey Vulture

Turkey Vultures, Black Vultures, Bald Eagles, and Ospreys are large birds that often soar high in the sky, particularly on windy days. To tell the difference between these species, the bird that soars with its wings raised in a "V" while making broad circles is likely a Turkey Vulture. They use their keen sense of smell to find fresh carcasses. Turkey Vultures are most often seen in Evergrene from fall through the springtime, after which they migrate north to their summer nesting sites as far away as southern Canada.

Warblers

Warblers are a family of small, migratory birds that are often difficult to identify. Of the approximately 40 species of Warblers that have been documented in Florida, eight have been observed in Evergrene – all during the fall, winter, and spring. Many species change from showy breeding plumages in the summer to more drab plumages in the winter. Several of the more common species are shown below. They are frequently found in oak and pine trees where they search for insects in crevices of rough-barked trees.

Black-and-white Warbler
This species is the only all black and white Warbler in Florida. They are often seen upside-down on tree trunks and branches as they search for insects. Black-and-white Warblers migrate south to Florida in the fall. In the late spring, they fly north to nesting sites as far away as central Canada.

Northern Parula
Northern Parulas are small, brightly colored Warblers that are found in south Florida from the fall through the spring. Parulas have a yellow throat, gray wings with double white wing bars, and a yellowish-green patch on their upper back. They often forage in flocks with other Warblers. Their high-pitched buzzy trill sometimes gives away their presence during the springtime when they prepare to migrate north to nesting locations from north Florida to northern Canada.

Ovenbird
These small Warblers (approximately 6 inches in length) have olive green backs, white undersides with black streaks, reddish crowns, and white rings around their eyes. Ovenbirds nest across most of the eastern U.S. during the summer and spend the rest of the year in Florida and other southern regions. Although uncommon in Evergrene, they sometimes can be found foraging for food in dense vegetation on the ground.

Palm Warbler

Palm Warblers have yellow or yellow-white undersides with rust coloring on top of their heads. They have a habit of constantly flicking their tails up and down, which helps to identify them. These insect-eating birds spend the fall through springtime in our area, and then they migrate north for the summer nesting season.

Pine Warbler

The double wing bars and lack of yellow on either the top or bottom of the tail help to distinguish Pine Warblers from other Warblers that winter in Evergrene and south Florida.

Prairie Warbler

Prairie Warblers are identified by the combination of bright-yellow chests and bellies, black streaks on their sides, and olive-green heads and backs.

Yellow-rumped Warbler

Yellow-rumped Warblers are the most common Warbler in Evergrene. When the yellow on the top of their rump is not visible, small yellow streaks on the birds' sides help identify them. In the summertime, they nest from the central U.S. to Alaska, and they return south for the fall through the springtime.

Downy Woodpecker

Less than 7 inches in length, Downy Woodpeckers are the smallest members of the Woodpecker family. They have black and white stripes on their heads, black wings with white spots, broad white stripes down the center of their backs, and white undersides. Males have red patches on the backs of their heads; females do not. Downy Woodpeckers are insect eaters and are most often found in forested areas where they nest in dead pine trees. This non-migratory species resides throughout North America. They are only occasionally seen in Evergrene.

Pileated Woodpecker

Pileated Woodpeckers are easily recognized by the bright red crest on the top of their heads. Their bodies are mostly black with white lines near their heads and necks. Males and females both have red crests, but only the males have a red "moustache" stripe. Pileated woodpeckers are the largest of the woodpeckers in Florida. They are not often seen in Evergrene.

Red-bellied Woodpecker

Red-bellied Woodpeckers are one of four species of insect-eating Woodpeckers that live in Evergrene. They are part of a sub-group of Woodpeckers called "Ladderbacks" because of the alternating dark and light ladder-like rungs on their backs. Approximately 10 inches in length, they are smaller than northern Flickers and Pileated Woodpeckers and larger than Downy Woodpeckers. Woodpeckers can stick out their barbed tongues nearly two inches past the end of their beak which makes it easier for them to snatch prey from deep crevices in tree bark.

Yellow-bellied Sapsucker

Yellow-bellied Sapsuckers are medium-sized Woodpeckers that are most easily identified by a white stripe that is visible on its wings, black and white stripes on its face, and a bright red patch on its head. These migratory birds nest in northern latitudes in the summertime across most of the U.S. and Canada. They can be found in Florida in the fall through the spring but have only been seen occasionally in Evergrene.

Raptors

Raptors, or birds of prey, are medium to large carnivorous birds that have hooked beaks and large sharp talons that they use to capture their prey. Several species of raptors, including Ospreys, Bald Eagles, and Snail Kites, are most often seen near the water or wetlands in Evergrene. Other raptors, including most Hawks and Owls, are more often observed in or near the northern preserves in Evergrene.

American Kestrel

The smallest and most common of the Falcon family, Kestrels are winter-time residents in Evergrene. They have two vertical black stripes on each side of their face which helps to identify them. Their shrill "killy, killy, killy" call often gives away their presence.

Bald Eagle

Bald Eagles are large birds of prey. Their white heads and tails make them easy to distinguish from the more abundant Turkey Vultures, Black Vultures, and Ospreys. Once in danger of extinction in the early 1960's, Bald Eagle populations rebounded after passage of the Federal Endangered Species Act in 1973 and the banning of the pesticide DDT. Florida has more nesting Bald Eagles than any other state except Alaska. Bald Eagles are most often seen circling high over Lake Dorothy looking for fish, which is their primary food. They are year-round residents in Florida.

Immature Bald Eagle

Adult Bald Eagle

Hawks

Broad-winged Hawk
The distinctive brown-and-white-streaked breasts of Broad-winged Hawks help differentiate them from the more commonly found Red-shouldered Hawks. Adult Broad-winged Hawks are about 13-19 inches tall, which is slightly smaller than Red-shouldered Hawks. During the summertime, they nest east of the Mississippi River from Georgia to southern Canada. Although infrequently seen in Evergrene, these hawks can occasionally be found here in the wintertime.

Red-shouldered Hawk
Red-shouldered Hawks are slightly smaller than Ospreys. The distinguishing feature of this species is the rusty reddish patch on their shoulders, which gives the Red-shouldered Hawk its name. Juveniles do not have reddish shoulders, but they do have the same overall streaked brown plumage of adults. These Hawks hunt for small mammals, reptiles, and amphibians. They are year-round residents in Evergrene and are most often found near wetland areas.

Owls

Eastern Screech Owl

Eastern Screech Owls are the smallest of five species of Owls that inhabit Florida. They are short stocky birds – only 8 to 10 inches in height – with large heads, short necks, rounded wings, pointed ear tufts, and yellow eyes. Screech Owls don't really screech, but you may hear their distinctive quavering whistling at night. Their gray-patterned intricate bands and spots make for excellent camouflage against tree bark. Several pairs of Screech Owls have taken up residence in nest boxes in Evergrene's wooded preserves.

Owlets in one of Evergrene's nest boxes

Great Horned Owl

Great Horned Owls are more than twice the size of Screech Owls. Their mottled gray-brown colors help them blend in with their surroundings, making them hard to find. They have distinctive feathered ear tufts and a hooting call often heard at night.

Osprey

Also known as "fish hawks," Ospreys are large raptors with dark wings and white undersides. They are almost always found near lakes, estuaries, and other open-water bodies. Many Ospreys are year-round residents in Florida. However, their population in Florida increases during the fall, winter, and spring when migrating Ospreys that nest in the north are in Florida. Evergrene installed a tall nesting platform along the eastern shore of Lake Dorothy to attract Ospreys and Bald Eagles.

Swallow-tailed Kite

The long forked tail and graceful flight pattern of Swallow-tailed Kites make them one of the most easily identified raptors in Evergrene. They arrive from southern latitudes in late February and early March for the spring and summer nesting season before returning south in the fall. They are occasionally seen over the preserves in the northern part Evergrene.

Other Evergrene Wildlife

In addition to birds, other animals make their homes in Evergrene. Some of them are pictured here.

Gopher Tortoise

Gopher Tortoises have a brown or gray shell with strong back legs and shovel-like front legs for digging. They live in sunny locations with well-drained sandy soil where they dig deep burrows for shelter. Their burrows also provide shelter for about 350 other species, including lizards, frogs, rabbits, and mice. Gopher Tortoises can live for 40 to 60 years. The shell of an adult Gopher Tortoise is typically 9 to 11 inches long. The average adult weighs about nine pounds. Gopher Tortoises are listed as threatened* under the Florida Wildlife Code, and, as such, they are protected under Florida state law. Several of Evergrene's preserves were set aside to protect Tortoises and their habitats.

Gopher Tortoise burrow

---

* "Threatened" means a species is likely to become endangered within the foreseeable future. "Endangered" means a species is in danger of extinction throughout all or most of its range.

Turtles

Florida Softshell Turtle and River Cooter

There are more than 20 species of Turtles that inhabit southeast Florida. Some live in the sea, and some in wetlands, including lakes, ponds, and rivers. Two species, Cooters and Florida Softshell Turtles, evolved to thrive in wetland areas. These two species can be found in Evergrene as they laze about along the shores of our lake, ponds, and wetlands. While Florida Softshell Turtles and River Cooters live in water, Gopher Tortoises, pictured on the previous page, do not. In the springtime, even turtles that typically inhabit wetlands will venture to nearby uplands to lay their eggs.

Florida Softshell Turtle

Note: If you find a turtle or a tortoise crossing the road, it is fine to help it get to the other side, but don't put it in the water.

River Cooter

Rabbits

Both Eastern Cottontails and their close relatives, Marsh Rabbits, can be found in Evergrene. Cottontails live in open areas and are most active around dusk or dawn. The less common Marsh Rabbits live in wetland habitats and often stay in the brush to avoid predators. The easiest way to tell these two species apart is by their tails. Eastern Cottontails have white tails, while Marsh Rabbits have small brown tails. Also, Cottontails are generally larger than Marsh Rabbits and have slightly lighter fur and larger ears.

Eastern Cottontail Rabbit

Marsh Rabbit

Brown Basilisk Lizard

Brown Basilisk Lizards have large hind feet with flaps of skin between their toes. They can move quickly across land and water. Their web-like feet give them the appearance of walking on water. Initially introduced from Central and South America to the Miami area in the 1970's, this invasive species has expanded its range throughout much of the southern half of Florida.

Squirrels

Eastern Gray Squirrel

Two species of squirrels inhabit the woodlands in Evergrene – Eastern Gray Squirrels and Southern Flying Squirrels. Eastern Gray Squirrels are by far the more common of the two species. They are often seen feeding on pine nuts and acorns or brazenly stealing food from bird feeders.

Southern Flying Squirrel

Southern Flying Squirrels are primarily nocturnal, so they are not seen very often. They are smaller than Gray Squirrels yet have relatively large eyes which helps their night vision. Flying Squirrels don't actually "fly." They have a furry membrane that extends between their front and rear legs that allows them to glide through the air from tree to tree. These squirrels have discovered that the nest boxes in Evergrene, which were built for birds, also make great homes to keep them cool, dry, and safe from predators.

Around Evergrene

Sunsets

Adults and children enjoy fishing along the shorelines of Lake Dorothy and other water bodies in Evergrene.

Rainbows

Double rainbow over Lake Dorothy

Appendix 1 – Map of Florida

Palm Beach Gardens, shown by the yellow asterisk above, is along south Florida's east coast, about 60 miles north of Miami and 260 miles south of Jacksonville.

Appendix 2 – Evergrene Map

Key

Nest Boxes (36)   *

Osprey Platform   ◻

Map Source: Google Earth
Date of photo: 1/13/2019

Appendix 3 – Evergrene Bird List
(*indicates birds included in this book)

American Bittern
American Coot*
American Goldfinch
American Kestrel*
American Redstart
American Robin
Anhinga*
Bald Eagle*
Baltimore Oriole
Black-necked Stilt*
Black Scoter
Black Skimmer
Black Vulture*
Black-and white Warbler*
Black-bellied Whistling Duck*
Black-throated Blue Warbler
Blue Jay*
Blue-gray Gnatcatcher*
Blue-headed Vireo
Blue-winged Teal*
Boat-tailed Grackle*
Bonaparte's Gull*
Broad-winged Hawk*
Brown Pelican*
Brown Thrasher*
Carolina Wren
Cattle Egret*
Cedar Waxwing*
Chimney Swift
Chuck-Will's-Widow
Common Gallinule*
Common Grackle*
Common Ground-Dove
Common Nighthawk
Common Yellowthroat
Cooper's Hawk
Double-crested Cormorant*
Downey Woodpecker*
Eastern Phoebe*

Eastern Screech Owl*
Eastern Towhee*
Egyptian Goose*
Eurasian Collared-Dove*
European Starling*
Fish Crow*
Forster's Tern
Glossy Ibis*
Gray Catbird*
Gray-headed Swamphen*
Great Blue Heron*
Great Crested Flycatcher*
Great Egret*
Great Horned Owl*
Greater Yellowlegs*
Green Heron*
House Sparrow*
Killdeer*
Kingfisher
Laughing Gull
Least Bittern*
Least Sandpiper*
Least Tern*
Lesser Scaup*
Lesser Yellowlegs
Limpkin*
Little Blue Heron*
Loggerhead Shrike*
Magnificent Frigatebird*
Mottled Duck*
Mourning Dove*
Northern Cardinal*
Northern Flicker
Northern Mockingbird*
Northern Parula*
Northern Shoveler*
Osprey*
Ovenbird*
Painted Bunting*

Palm Warbler*
Pied-billed Grebe*
Pileated Woodpecker*
Pine Warbler*
Prairie Warbler*
Purple Gallinule*
Purple Martin*
Red-bellied Woodpecker*
Red-eyed Vireo*
Red-shouldered Hawk*
Red-tailed Hawk
Red-winged Blackbird*
Ring-billed Gull*
Ring-necked Duck*
Rose-breasted Grosbeak
Roseate Spoonbill*
Royal Tern
Ruby-throated Hummingbird*
Ruddy Duck*
Sandhill Crane*
Short-tailed Hawk
Snail Kite
Snowy Egret*
Solitary Sandpiper*
Swallow-tailed Kite*
Tree Swallow
Tricolored Heron*
Turkey Vulture*
Whip-poor-will
White Ibis*
White-eyed Vireo*
White-winged Dove*
Wilson's Snipe*
Wood Duck*
Wood Stork*
Yellow-bellied Sapsucker*
Yellow-rumped Warbler*
Yellow-throated Warbler

Appendix 4 – Birding Etiquette*

Respect and promote birds and their environment.

Support the conservation of birds and their habitats. Engage in and promote bird-friendly practices, such as keeping pets indoors or controlled, maintaining safe and clean feeding stations, and landscaping with native plants.

Avoid stressing birds or exposing them to danger. Be particularly cautious around active nests and feeding sites. Always exercise caution and restraint when photographing, recording, or otherwise approaching birds.

Minimize habitat disturbance. Stay on sidewalks and trails.

Respect and promote the birding community and its members.

Respect the interests of fellow birders and outdoor enthusiasts. Freely share your knowledge and experience and be especially helpful to beginning birders.

Share bird observations freely, as birders derive considerable benefit from publicly available bird sightings.

In group birding situations, ensure that the group does not unduly interfere with others using the same area.

Respect and promote the laws and the rights of others.

Never enter private property without the owner's permission.

Familiarize yourself with and follow all laws, rules, and regulations governing activities at your birding location. In particular, be aware of regulations related to species that are threatened or endangered, and do not disturb nesting areas or sensitive habitats.

Birding should be fun and help build a better future for birds, birders, and all people. Birders should always give back more than they take.

---

*Excerpts from the American Birding Association's Code of Birding Ethics (https://www.aba.org/aba-code-of-birding-ethics/)

Appendix 5 – Attracting and Feeding Birds

In addition to the birds that are naturally attracted to the wetlands and preserves in Evergrene, there are other ways that residents can attract birds, such as by planting and maintaining a variety of native plants. Many of the native plants that are used for landscaping in Evergrene were specifically selected for their desirability as habitats for birds as well as for bearing fruit, berries, and seeds that birds eat. The University of Florida's Institute of Food and Agricultural Sciences (IFAS) produces a variety of peer-reviewed papers on this subject. A good place to start is https://edis.ifas.ufl.edu/uw384.

Suggestions for plantings that are specifically designed to attract hummingbirds in Florida can be found at: https://gardeningsolutions.ifas.ufl.edu/design/types-of-gardens/hummingbird-gardens.html.

Growing native plants that attract birds and other wildlife is preferable to installing and maintaining bird feeders. Among other benefits, native plants provide natural foods and are less likely to attract undesirable species. Recommended native plants for Evergrene's zip code can be found at: https://www.audubon.org/native-plants.

In 2002, the Florida Fish and Wildlife Conservation Commission made it illegal to intentionally feed sandhill cranes (Florida Administrative Code 68A-4.001(6)). There are many reasons why sandhill cranes should not be fed by humans. Not only is it illegal to feed them, but Florida sandhill cranes have an abundant supply of natural foods to eat, such as insects and small animals. They do not need handouts from humans. For the good of the cranes, please do not feed them.

- When cranes are fed and learn to associate people with food, they can lose their fear of humans. These "habituated" cranes may approach people and even grab food out of a person's hand. In rare instances, cranes have been reported pecking people.
- Cranes also have been known to damage window screens and other property. This behavior is probably a response of the birds seeing their reflection, which brings out territorial defense behaviors such as scratching at windows or shiny automobiles.
- Cranes attracted to people's yards for food are put at risk as they walk across roads. Many sandhill cranes are killed each year on Florida roads.
- Attracting cranes to urban areas increases the threat of attack (especially to young cranes) by dogs, cats or other domestic animals.
- Additionally, the cranes' diet, which normally is quite diverse, is disrupted when they eat one food item (e.g., corn) consistently.

Endangered Species

It is against Florida law to feed any bird listed on the state's endangered or threatened list. A species that has been designated as "threatened" or "endangered" means that the species is struggling to survive. The species designated as "threatened" that are listed in this book include little blue herons, tricolored herons, roseate spoonbills, sandhill cranes, and gopher tortoises. A complete list of Florida's imperiled species can be found at: https:myfwc.com/wildlifehabitats/wildlife/plan/

Appendix 6 – Bird Calls, Songs, and Noises

Most bird species have a wide repertoire of songs and calls. Some (e.g., sandhill cranes – https:www.allaboutbirds.org/guide/Sandhill_Crane/) are easily identifiable. Others, particularly migratory birds that are in Florida during their non-nesting season, are mostly silent, as they are not establishing and defending territories or extensively communicating with one another or their young.

Even within a species, there is a large diversity of bird sounds, which may vary depending on the time of year. During the nesting season, bird songs are at their peak. For many species, males' songs are important in establishing and defending territories and attracting mates. Parents communicate with young, but not in the melodious songs associated with the nesting season.

Some of most familiar bird calls heard in Evergrene include the piercing cries of limpkins, especially at night (https://www.allaboutbirds.org/guide/Limpkin/sounds), the guttural squawks of many of the wading birds, and even the ubiquitous calls of boat-tailed grackles at the clubhouse (https://www.allaboutbirds.org/guide/Boat-tailed_Grackle/).

Some birds at Evergene (e.g., catbirds) are more often heard than seen, as they are usually in areas of dense vegetation. Their cat-like calls, which tell us they are here even when we can't see them, are far less melodious than the songs of this same species during the nesting season. Catbirds are in the same bird family as mockingbirds, which get their name from their ability to "mock" or copy the sounds of many other species. Mockingbirds keep up with the times and can mimic cell phone ringtones, car alarms, and other familiar noises.

Some birds (e.g., those annoying woodpeckers!) communicate with one another with non-vocal noises, which sometimes prompt comments like "Why is that darn woodpecker tapping on my metal downspout?" Male woodpeckers have figured out that if they tap on something metal, the reverberations carry over a much larger area than if they tap on wood or a rotting tree. This is the bird's way of trying to establish and defend a larger nesting territory and attract a mate from farther away.

A few birds can even be identified by the sounds of their wings. Unlike owls, which are notably quiet in flight, mourning doves have a noticeable "wingword" (https://www.allaboutbirds.org/guide/Mourning_Dove/sounds).

If bird calls interest you, search around on the web. The Cornell Laboratory of Ornithology (https://www.birds.cornell.edu/home/) and https://www.bird-sounds.net/alphabetical/ have short recordings of all bird species found in North America. Merlin Bird ID is an excellent and easy-to-use app by the Cornell Lab of Ornithology. It can be used to identify bird species by photos or by the sounds of their calls. This app is available to download for free from the app store on your phone.

References

Many excellent field guides, websites, apps and other reference materials are available to help identify and learn about birds. Some of these are listed below.

Books and Journals

1. The National Geographic Society's Field Guide to the Birds of North America, J.L. Dunn and J. Alderfer, 2017 – Seventh Edition, National Geographic Society, Washington D.C., 591 pp.
2. Smithsonian Handbooks, Birds of Florida, F. Alsop, 2002, DK Publishing, Inc., 399 pp.
3. The Sibley Guide to Birds, 2nd Edition, D.A. Sibley, 2014, Alfred A. Knopf Publisher, 624 pp.
4. National Audubon Society Field Guide to North American Birds: Eastern Region, Revised Edition, 2021, National Audubon Society, Knopf Publishing, 912 pp.
5. "First Documented Nesting in the Wild of Egyptian Geese in Florida," by Greg Braun, Florida Field Naturalist, Vol. 32, No. 4, November 2004, published by the Florida Ornithological Society, pp. 138-143, http://sustainableecosystemsinternational.com/wp-content/uploads/2013/06/FL-Field-Naturalist-Egyptian-Geese-Vol-32-No-4.pdf

Websites

6. Cornell Laboratory of Ornithology –https://www.birds.cornell.edu/home/
7. eBird, discover a new world of birding at ebird.org
8. birdweb.org/birdweb/resources
9. fl.audubon.org
10. Local Audubon chapter: Audubon Everglades, https://www.auduboneverglades.org
11. The American Birding Association, www.aba.org

About the Authors

Originally from New York and then Maryland, Alan Rubin has been a resident of Evergrene since 2016. He is a retired engineer and an amateur photographer who specializes in photographing nature and birds. Alan frequently contributes bird photos to "Our Evergrene," the community's quarterly magazine. His photos have appeared on the cover of the magazine six times. Alan published another bird book in 2020 entitled "All About Robins," which is available on Amazon.com.

Alan Rubin taking photos alongside one of Evergrene's ponds

Greg Braun is a professional ecologist with over 30 years of experience in natural ecosystems in Florida, the southeastern United States, the Bahamas and the Caribbean. A Certified Environmental Professional, Greg is the owner of Sustainable Ecosystems International, an ecological consulting firm based in Jupiter, Florida. Greg has conducted bird surveys in Evergrene since 2003 as part of Evergrene's initial certification and annual recertifications in Audubon International's Cooperative Sanctuary Program. Greg has also taught bird identification classes for Audubon and at Evergrene. See more at SustainableEcosystemsInternational.com.

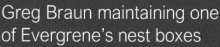

Greg Braun maintaining one of Evergrene's nest boxes

Made in United States
Orlando, FL
15 December 2024

54949749R10044